The Healthy Parent's ABC's

Healthy Parenting
Made Clear and Easy-to-Read

Benjamin D. Garber, PhD

UNHOOKED BOOKS
An Imprint of High Conflict Institute Press
Scottsdale, Arizona

D1225452

Publisher's Note
This publication is designed to provide accurate and authoritative information about the subject matter covered. It is sold with the understanding that neither the author nor publisher are rendering legal, mental health, medical, or other professional services, either directly or indirectly. If expert assistance, legal services, or counseling is needed, the services of a competent professional should be sought. Neither the author nor the publisher shall be liable or responsible for any loss or damage allegedly arising as a consequence of your use or application of any information or suggestions in this book.

Copyright © 2015 by Benjamin D. Garber
Unhooked Books, LLC
7701 E. Indian School Rd., Ste. F
Scottsdale, AZ 85251
www.unhookedbooks.com

ISBN: 978-1-936268-99-3

Cover design by Kristen Onesti

Printed in the United States of America

ALSO BY BENJAMIN D. GARBER

Letting Go—Holding Tight: Raising Healthy Children in Troubled Times (2016)

Keeping Kids Out of the Middle (2008)

Developmental Psychology for Family Law Professionals (2009)

Ten Child-Centered Forensic Family Evaluation Tools (2015)

The Parenting Plan Workbook (2015)

ABOUT THE AUTHOR

Ben Garber is a husband, son and the father of two. He is a New Hampshire licensed psychologist, a former Guardian ad litem and a Parenting Coordinator. He is an invited speaker and professional trainer across the United States and Canada, a prolific writer and a closet cartoonist.

Dr. Garber has advanced degrees in child and family development, clinical psychology, and psycholinguistics from the Pennsylvania State University and the University of Michigan. He has lived and worked in New Hampshire since 1988, opening his present practice in clinical child, family, forensic and consulting psychology in 1999. When not engaged in professional activities or involved with family matters, Dr. Garber can often be found kayaking and fishing on the remote lakes and rivers of Northern New England and occasionally scuba diving in warmer waters to the south.

Dr. Garber is a nationally renowned speaker, researcher and an award winning freelance journalist, writing in the areas of child and family development for popular press publications appearing around the world and in juried professional publications in both law and psychology.

HOW TO USE THIS BOOK

Healthy parenting doesn't require a college diploma or a vocabulary full of psychobabble. It doesn't require special classes or expensive professionals. Healthy parenting requires that you master some basics. This book introduces those basics in simple, clear language.

Twenty-six letters A through Z. Start today by making this week "A week." Talk every day about how you can be a better ANCHOR for your kids. Next week is "B week," an opportunity to talk about BATTLES and how to avoid them. Moving forward one letter per week, you'll complete the entire alphabet twice in each year. The process is fun and important and painless and free and entirely to the benefit of your children.

Daycares and preschools, Sunday Schools and elementary schools, scout troops and dance studios and everywhere that children are found, parents can learn the HealthyParent's ABCs.

I am my child's Anchor

I am my child's anchor.

I am stable and calm.
No matter how big the storm,
no matter how crazy life becomes,
I connect my child to solid ground.

When my child gets mad, I stay calm.
I can show him how to be angry without hurting.

When my child is sad, I stay calm.
I can hold her and comfort her.

When my child is scared, I stay calm.
I can make sure that he is safe and
I can help him to feel safe.

When my child is happy,
I can be happy with her.

READ MORE ABOUT
MAD • "NO!" • Routines

How can I be a better Anchor?

I can take good care of myself.

If I am healthy, I am a good anchor.
If I am healthy, I am a good model for my child to copy.

I can make good choices.

I am healthy if I am drug-free and alcohol-free.
I am healthy if I have good friends to talk to.
I am healthy when I eat well and exercise every day.

I am healthy if I can say "NO" calmly and firmly.

I can talk about my feelings.

I can say, "I feel mad!"
I can say, "I feel sad!"
I can say, "I feel scared!"

READ MORE ABOUT
Grandparents · Emotions

Battles happen

Some battles are worth fighting.
Most battles are not.

Children invite battles. Kids fuss and yell a lot.
They say "NO!" often. Should I argue? Should I battle?

Sometimes the battle isn't important.
Sometimes I can ignore the fussing and yelling.
When the battle isn't important, its okay to let it go.

When the battle is important,
I must be firm.

Everything about safety is important:
We must always ride in car seats or wear seat belts.
Children must wear bike and scooter helmets.
Children must never play with matches or electric.
Children must never play with chemicals.

Safety is always worth the battle.

READ MORE ABOUT
NO! · Mad!

What can I do when my child

Battles me?

"Sammy, its time for bed!" "No!"What can I do now?

1. Ignore her.
Is she just trying to make me mad? Don't battle.
I will stay calm and keep moving to her bedroom.

2. Be silly.
"Can you hop to your bed like a bunny?"
"Watch me hop to your bed like a bunny!"

3. Distract her.
"Did you see the stars outside your window?"
"How many stuffed animals are in your bed?"

4. Bribe her.
"If you can get in bed, then you can pick your story!"
"If you can get to your bed before me,
then I'll give you a tickle!"

READ MORE ABOUT
Consistency · **Follow through**

onsistency
Kids keeps calm

Consistency means stable.

Consistency means predictable.

Consistency means that I am predictable.
When I am predictable, My kids can learn
how to succeed.

Routines create consistency.
Routines help to keep my kids and families calm.

One bedtime routine goes like this:
First we eat supper.
Then we take a bath.
Next we put on pajamas.
In bed for story.
One kiss. One hug. Night-night!

When I am consistent, my kids will be calmer
and everyone will be happier.

READ MORE ABOUT
Routine · **G**randparents · **O**pen communication

But **Consistent**
is boring!

My son is like a car. When his gas
tank is empty, he breaks down.

Consistency and routines are like coasting downhill.
My son needs very little gas because I have made
everything consistent. He can save his gas for
learning and growing and playing.

Change can be upsetting.
Change can make kids mad and
sad and scared and happy!

Change is like driving uphill. It takes a lot of gas.

My kids have less gas for learning and growing
and playing when there is too much change.

READ MORE ABOUT
Healthy • **If ... then** • **Follow through**

6

Divorce

ends an adult–adult relationship. It must never end a parent-child relationship

Separation and divorce happen.

Sometimes continuing an adult-adult relationship is destructive.

Living apart or divorcing may end the adult-adult battles but each parent-child relationship must go on.

I know that my child's relationship with his other parent is separate from my relationship with my child's other parent.

I must keep my feelings for my child's other parent away from my child.

I must allow my child to love his other parent even if I don't.

READ MORE ABOUT
Grandparents · Routine · Mad

7

But he's always putting me

Down!

A parent who interferes with a child's love for another parent is being selfish, angry and immature.

I know that my child must be free to feel about his other parent any way that he feels.

I know that if my child is happy or sad or mad or scared about his other parent, I can support him no matter how I feel about that person myself.

I know that if I believe that another parent has put me down to my child, I must talk to the other parent directly and privately.

I know that putting a child in the middle of an adult-adult battle or asking a child to chose between beloved parents hurts the child.

# Emotions

I know that every day everyone feels
Happy
Sad
Mad
Scared

I know that its healthy to feel these emotions.

I know that it is unhealthy to try to hold my emotions inside.

I know that there are okay ways to express these feelings. I know there are other ways to express these feelings that are not okay.

I know that the only way that my kids can learn that it is okay to have feelings is by my example.

I know that the only way that my kids can learn how to express their feelings is by my example.

READ MORE ABOUT
Mad

Emotions

are like air inside a balloon.
If I don't let them out, I'll explode

How can I teach my children to let their feelings out safely?

1. When my child uses words to tell me how he feels, I say, "Thanks for telling me."

2. I try to label what I think my child may be feeling so that he can learn to do the same: "You look pretty mad, Timmy!"

3. I try to show my child how to let his emotional pressure out so that he won't be dangerous or destructive.

4. When my child is dangerous or destructive, I try to help him learn what he should differently next time.

What to do?
Punch a pillow • Yell in an empty milk jug
Rip up newspaper • Scribble on newspaper
Jump up and down • Pound Play-doh • Draw a picture
Exercise • Talk about it

READ MORE ABOUT
Safety

10

Follow through

I know that when I do as I say
my kids know what to expect
and will listen better.

I know that when I say one thing but don't follow
through, my kids feel confused and uncertain
and won't listen to me next time.

I know that nagging or saying one thing over
and over and over teaches my kids that I don't
mean what I say and teaches my kids not to listen.

I know that if its worth saying and
if I want my kids to do as I ask, then I should say it
once and only once and then follow through.

READ MORE ABOUT
Battles • **If**...then • **O**pen communication

He never listens to me!

I know that I have to teach my children how to listen to me and do as I say.

I know that my children will never learn to listen and do as I say if I don't follow through.

I know that if I want her to learn to listen, I need to ask this way every single time:

"Sarah?"
(I make sure that she's looking at me)
"Its time to turn the TV off now"
(I say my expectation clearly and calmly)
"If the TV is off, we can go out and play"
(I offer a positive if...then first)
"If the TV stays on, then I'll have to turn it off and there will be no TV after school today."
(I offer a negative if...then last)

READ MORE ABOUT
Consistency • Routine

Grandparents
and other parenting partners

I know that parenting can be exhausting.
I know that if I'm exhausted, I won't think
clearly or give fully to my kids.

I know that I need parenting partners
to raise the healthiest child possible.

I know that my child's other parent,
my child's grandparents, my brothers
and sisters and neighbors and friends
all might be excellent parenting partners.

I know that healthy parenting partners:
1. Talk often and openly about the child's needs
2. Work together as a team to meet the child's needs
3. Never put each other down in front of the child
4. Always respect each other's parenting decisions

READ MORE ABOUT
Divorce · **F**ollow through · **C**onsistency · **R**outine

13

But Granny lets me do that!

I know children sometimes try to split between parenting partners. They sometimes try to make me feel like a bad parent to get their own way.

I know that if my child complains, "But Granny let's me do that!" then first I need to check with Granny.

I know that healthy parenting partners try to be consistent and try to keep up the same rules and expectations.

The best solution is to communicate with my parenting partners to work out the difference.

Why does Granny do it one way? Why do I do it a different way? Should I change? Should she? Can we compromise?

If we can't agree then its still okay to say to my child, "That's the way you do it with Granny. This is the way you do it with me."

READ MORE ABOUT
Open communication

Healthy
is more important
than happy

**If I am a healthy parent then I have
to make lots of hard choices.**

"Mommy, can I have more cake?"

"But Billy can cross the street, why can't I?"

"Just this once, Mommy. Please …!"

"If you don't let me then I hate you!"

**I must always make healthy choices,
even if my choices make my child mad.**

A healthy child has firm rules.

A healthy child eats and sleeps well.

A healthy child is safe.

A healthy child is supervised.

Its okay if he's mad, its okay if he's sad,
as long as he's healthy.

I'm his parent. I don't need to be his friend.

When my child is healthy, he has a chance to be happy.

**READ MORE ABOUT
Mad!**

15

But its easier when he's

Happy!

I can give in to his whining and crying and now and have some peace and quiet.

I know that when I give in, I'm teaching him to whine and cry more!

If I'm firm and calm now, he'll learn that whining and crying don't work.

"But sometimes I can't take it!"
I'm only human. I have my limits.
When I can't take any more, I can't give in.

I CAN ask for help From my parenting partners.

Hugs help. Hitting hurts.

helps my kids make better choices

"If … then" makes the world predictable.
"If … then" tells my kids what will
happen next.

I say, "If you sit down, then we will watch TV."
If he sits down, then I turn the TV on.
If he doesn't sit down, then the TV stays off.

I say, "If you use your words, then I can help you."

I say, "If you hit me, then you'll have a time out."

I know that if I use make an "if … then" statement then
I must follow through.

I know that if I make an "if … then" statement and
I do not follow through, then my kids have no reason
to do as I say.

READ MORE ABOUT
Follow through • Consistency • Time out

17

If you make good choices...then I can reward you

I know that rewards are more powerful than punishments. I know that it is easier to punish a problem than it is to reward a success.

Problems are louder than successes.

If I try, then I can catch my child succeeding every day.

I know that if I catch my child succeeding and if I reward my child's successes, then my child will feel proud and happy and he will try harder to succeed.

I know that if I only punish the problem behaviors, I may be teaching my child to misbehave.

READ MORE ABOUT
Open communication • Punishment

Juggling
is a necessary
parenting skill

I know that a healthy parent must be able to juggle.

I know that I have to be able to
wash the clothes
make the supper
answer the phone
pay the bills
cuddle one child and
color with another
all at once even when I'm hungry and tired and sick.

I know that I have to be able to say "No" to some people about some things some times to raise a healthy child.

I know that I must know my own limits. I know that I must get myself refueled if I want to be able to refuel my kids.

READ MORE ABOUT
Grandparents • "NO!"

Joking can be fun.
Teasing can be painful.

A joke is something that we can all laugh
at without hurting anyone's feelings:
"Who lives next door to the horse?"
"His neighhhhh-bor!"

Teasing makes some people laugh and other
people cry, even if their tears are invisible.
Name-calling and bullying, taunting and
harassing are forms of teasing.

Healthy parents make sure that humor
is a part of every day.

Healthy parents can laugh at
themselves and their mistakes and,
In so doing, teach children the same skill.

READ MORE ABOUT
Mad · **O**pen communication · **E**motion

20

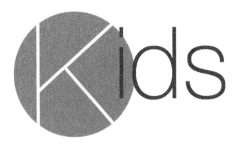

Kids

Kids are what being a parent is all about

I know that my kids will
bruise me
aggravate me
scare me
exhaust me
shock me
please me
abandon me
sadden me
embarrass me
and make me proud sometimes all at once.

I know that I must slowly let my kids go further and further away.

I know that I am a launching pad and, if I am a healthy parent, my kids will launch themselves into their own healthy adulthood.

READ MORE ABOUT
Anchors

Kids are not just little adults

I know that my kids think and feel and see and hear in kid ways.

I know that play is the work that my kids do to understand the world they live in.

I know that something I see as unimportant could be my kid's greatest treasure.

I know that some things that I see as important are probably meaningless to my kids I know that my genuine attention and sincere acceptance and caring mean more to my kids than gold.

I know that to be a healthy parent I must allow myself to be a little kid sometimes.

READ MORE ABOUT
Understand

Love is constant.

Love is no matter what.

My love for my kids never goes away. Its always there, even when I'm mad.

Mad is NOT the opposite of love.

I know that my kids will test my love. I know that my kids need to hear and see and feel my love often, especially when I'm mad or sad or scared.

I love my kids for who they are. I love my kids no matter what. I love my kids even when I'm mad at their choices.

I show my kids my love with hugs and kisses and cuddles. I show my kids my love by giving them my time and attention and caring.

I know that if I love my kids no matter what, then they can learn to love themselves and some day they will love their children no matter what.

READ MORE ABOUT
Anchors • Health

23

Parent-child **love** is different than adult-adult love

The love between two adults can break.

The love between a parent and a child can never break.

The love between two adults is a two-way street. each adult gives to the other.

The love between a parent and a child is a one-way street.

The parent gives to the child expecting nothing in return.

When the love between two adults breaks (when a couple breaks up or divorces) each adult can still love the kids and the kids must be allowed to keep loving each adult.

READ MORE ABOUT
Divorce • **G**randparents • **O**pen communication

Mad

is natural and normal and necessary.

Everyone feels mad sometimes.

Everyone feels happy and sad and scared, too.

My kids will feel mad sometimes. I know that's okay. It's my job to teach my kids how to let out their mad feelings without hurting me or themselves.

It's my job to show my kids that mad does not stop love.
It is okay to be mad.
It is not okay to hurt living things.
It's not okay to hit or kick or bite.
It's not okay to break toys.

I must decide if it is okay to ...
...   scream into an empty milk jug?
...   hit a pillow?
...   scribble a mad picture?
...   use words to say, "I'm mad!"

READ MORE ABOUT
Emotions

 How I show my anger teaches my kids how to show their anger

I know that if I swear and hit and hurt, my kids will learn to swear and hit and hurt.

If I hide my feelings in drinking or drugs, I know that my kids will learn to hide their feelings in drinking and drugs.

If I can say how I feel clearly, if I can control my temper if I stay clean and sober, I know that my kids can do the same.

And if my kids can say,
"I'm mad at you" …

First, I say, "Thank you for telling me."
Then we can talk about why they are mad
and what to do about it.

READ MORE ABOUT
Kids

When kids say,  "No!"

I know that my child has to say "No!"

I know that when my child says "NO!"
I do not have to battle with him.

I could punish him.

"Its time for school, Jonny!"
"NO!"
"Get in that car or no snack for you!"
but punishment feeds anger.

I know its better to distract him.
"Its time for school, Jonny!" "NO!"
"I wonder what snack will be this morning…?"

I know that sometimes I can reward him.
"Its time for school, Jonny!" "NO!"
"I've got a cookie for you when you're in your car seat!"

READ MORE ABOUT
Mad! • **J**uggling • **P**unishment

When I say,  "No!"

I know that I must say "No!"

I know that I must make rules and set limits to keep my child healthy.

I know that my kids will always test my rules and limits. I know that my kids need to discover that my rules and limits are firm and consistent.

My kids need to know that my rules and limits are a safety net that will always catch them.

I know that I must say "No!" firmly and clearly and consistently.

When kids say, N "No!"

READ MORE ABOUT
Follow through · **C**onsistency
Health · **A**nchor

Open
communication
builds trust

I know that I must talk to my parenting partners.

Some parents drop their child off and pick their child up from daycare or preschool or class with hardly a word.

I know that I need to talk to my child's caregivers and teachers and coaches and babysitters about his successes and failures, friends and enemies, health and habits, needs and wants and fears.

I need to tell them what I think and feel and I need to hear what they think and feel so that together we weave a safety net he can never fall through.

READ MORE ABOUT
Grandparents • Follow through • "No!"

Secrets and lies damage trust

I know that my parenting partners need to know everything about my child in order to meet my child's needs.

If I keep secrets from my parenting partners, then they can't meet my child's needs. If I lie to my parenting partners, then I will lose their trust and my child may lose their care.

I know that I must never ask my child to keep a secret from someone she loves. Keeping a secret for a young child is like asking her to carry a brick.

The secret becomes too heavy very quickly and has to be shared.

Lying to my child will lose her trust and teach her to lie to me in return.

READ MORE ABOUT
Consistency

Punishment
is always my last choice

When I respond to my child's behavior with harsh words
or by taking something away I am punishing him.

When my child learns what behavior gets punished,
he will do that behavior less often because he's scared.

Punishment builds anger and fear and shame.

But...
When I respond to my child's behavior
with pride or praise or gifts
I am rewarding him.

When my child learns what behavior gets rewarded,
he will do that behavior more often.

Rewards build pride and happiness and more successes.

READ MORE ABOUT
Mad! • Respect

When I reward good behavior there is less need for Punishment

Its easy to notice bad choices.

Its harder to notice good choices.

When I take the time to notice my child's good choices and successes I can reward these with praise and attention.

When José plays quietly while I read I make sure to tell him, "You're doing great there, buddy!" and "Thanks so much for letting me do my work!"

I know that if I don't reward his good behavior, he'll find something that is not okay to do, just to get my attention.

I know that if I reward my child's good choices, then my child will make more and more good choices and I won't need to punish him.

READ MORE ABOUT
Battles • If … then

Quality time

I know that what matters to my child is not HOW MUCH time we spend together but HOW GOOD the time is that we spend together.

I know that my
work and
cleaning and
shopping and
friends and family
all pull me away from my kids.

I try to spend as much quality time with them as I can.

Quality time means that I'm not distracted. I don't answer the phone or read the paper. Quality time means that my thoughts and feelings are focused on her no matter how long.

READ MORE ABOUT
Grandparents

Quality time
refuels my kids' emotional gas tank

I know that the hardest time of day can be when we first get home.

My child has been at school all day. I've been at work all day. A million chores are waiting to be done, but her emotional gas tank is empty.

I know that if I set aside ten minutes for cuddles and play to refuel her as soon as we get home, the rest of the night is easier for us both.

I know that if I don't make my time with my child important, she can't feel important.

I know that when I make my time with my child valuable she knows that she is valuable.

READ MORE ABOUT
Routines • Anchors

Routines

I know that when the world is calm and consistent my child feels secure and confident.

Routines make my child's world calm and consistent.
Routines make the world familiar.

A routine means that we always do
one thing first, then the next
then the last in order the same way every time.

A bedtime routine could be
First we eat supper
then we take a bath
next we read quietly in bed
then we kiss goodnight,
last is lights out.

Routines can help children Feel less nervous and scared.

READ MORE ABOUT
Consistency • Anchors

 Starting a new routine is hard.
Keeping up a familiar routine is easy.

I know that children battle against change.

Their battles get bigger and louder and more important as they get older.

I know that it may be hard to start a new routine today, but it will be even harder to start a new routine tomorrow.

I know that I can make our new routine into a song to help her learn it faster.

I know that if I want our new routine to work then all of my parenting partners must follow the same routine.

READ MORE ABOUT
Grandparents · "No!" · Open communication

afety
always comes first

My children must always be safe.

I will not allow my kids to do something that I believe is dangerous.

My kids are always supervised by a responsible adult. My kids are never allowed near fire or weapons, chemicals or medicine, open water or open windows.

My kids must use a car seat or a seat belt to ride in a car and never sit in the front with an air bag.

My kids must wear a helmet to ride a tricycle, a bicycle or scooter.

I keep medicine and matches, weapons and chemicals locked up and far away from my kids.

I make certain that babysitters and teachers know how to reach me at all times.

READ MORE ABOUT
Grandparents • Open communication

37

I expect fun but prepare for crisis

My children must always be safe!
I know how to dial 9 -1-1 for emergencies. I can teach my kids to dial 9-1-1 as soon as they're old enough.

Just in case
I keep a change of clothing, bandages and wipes in the car.

I know that my family doctor, pediatrician or nurse practitioner can answer all of my questions about health and safety.

I know that there are no stupid questions about safety.

And if my safety rules make my kids mad? Then we'll work on the mad feelings But the safety rules never change.

READ MORE ABOUT
Mad! • Health

Time out is not a punishment

Time out is a chance to cool off.

Time out is an invitation to chill out.

Time out is a way to help your kids settle down and avoid problems.

I give a time out because
I can see a problem coming.

Time out gives my kids a chance to stop and think and make better choices.

Time out works for everyone.
When I take a time out to cool off I'm teaching my kids to do the same.

Time out means
Breath, think, make careful choices.

READ MORE ABOUT
Battles • **If** ... then

How does Time out really work?

1. IF I see or hear my child getting wild being crazy revving up.

2. THEN I offer one warning, "Michael, its time to slow down."

3. IF he doesn't slow down himself, THEN I say quietly and firmly, "Let's do a time out, buddy."

4. He goes or I gently help him to a quiet, comfortable spot.

5. I congratulate him for getting there: "Good work, buddy. I'll let you know when you're all set."

6. I sit nearby and read quietly. I'll let him sit for 2 or 3 minutes until he's cooled off.

7. When he's cooled off, I say, "Great work, Michael!"

READ MORE ABOUT
Punishment

I take the time to try to Understand my kids

Children are not small adults.
They think and feel and talk and move differently.

Young children think about me-here-now.
I can't expect them to share and understand my feelings.

My young child's feelings can be sudden and intense.
My little boy or girl can be happy one second and crying or angry or scared the next.

Young children are just learning to talk. Parents and teachers and older kids must help them put their thoughts and feelings in to words.

Little kids drop things. They fall down often.
They are just learning to control their arms and legs, to control their peeing and pooping.

I can help my kids learn to think and feel, talk and move in more grown-up ways one step at a time.

READ MORE ABOUT
Kids

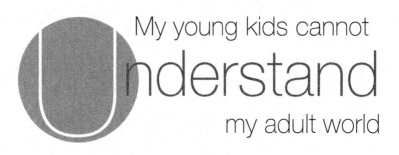

My young kids cannot Understand my adult world

Because my kids think and feel and talk and move differently, I know that I must protect them from the media.

Young children can be confused and scared by
the television news, violent pictures and words.

I know that my kids don't understand time.
One hour to my three year old is like one month to me.

I know that one angry word can feel to my five year old
the way a raging argument feels to me

I know that my kids understand me best when I am
calm and speak slowly and say one thing at a time.

READ MORE ABOUT
Violence

Violence
has no place in my child's life

I know that my kids copy what they see.

I know that my kids copy my behavior. If I hurt myself,
hurt other people or damage property, then I know that
they will do the same.

I know that my kids copy what they see on TV. If they see
people hurting animals or people, disrespecting people,
burning or breaking things, or using weapons
then I know that they will do the same.

I know that my kids copy what they see and hear. If I
allow them to witness violence among friends, family or
neighbors, on video games and in movies, then they will
copy what they have seen.

I know that if my children see me respect others and express my strong feelings appropriately then they will do the same.

READ MORE ABOUT
Kid • **U**nderstanding

43

Violence
has no place in parenting

Hitting
spanking
slapping
pushing
is NOT parenting. It is NOT punishing

IT IS ABUSE.

Punishing my child with violence might change his behavior.

But punishing my child with violence teaches fear and teaches violence.

Punishing my child with violence will change his behavior briefly, but will not give him better choices for next time.

Punishing my child with violence may scare him quiet or scare him away, but I want my child close by and able to tell me anything.

READ MORE ABOUT
Punishment

"Why?"

I know that my kids learn by asking questions.

Factual questions are invitations to learn and explore.
"Why is rain wet?"
"Why are trees green?"
"Why is cereal crunchy?"

I know its okay to say, "I don't know...
let's find out together."

Emotional questions usually need listening and caring more than answers.

"Why are you and daddy divorced?"
"Why do I have to go to the doctor?"
"Why are you so mad, mommy?"
I know I can answer these with a feeling word first,
"You sound pretty sad."
"I guess you're kind of scared, huh?"
"Don't worry, sweetie, everything's okay."

READ MORE ABOUT
Kids · **U**nderstanding

I try to hear the feelings in everything she says

If I get it wrong, she'll ask again later.

"No ...really, daddy, why are you divorced? "Yeah but why do I have to go...?" "Are you mad at me, mommy?"

Some "why" questions are an effort to avoid something.

"Time for bed, Niki!" "Why do I have to go, mama?"

"Eat up those peas, Michael!" "Why ?"

I know I can ignore some "why" questions. I know that if I try to explain, I'm inviting an argument.

Best to be firm and calm and say very little.

"I'm waiting, Niki.." "We can talk about that tomorrow."

READ MORE ABOUT
Emotions

46

X-rated

I know that some DVDs and videos are rated X to warn me that the movie is not healthy for children.

Many other things should be rated X
Because they are unhealthy for young children.

Some news programs are unhealthy for my kids.

Some music lyrics are unhealthy for my kids.

Some newspaper photos and
video games and adult conversations and
adult activities should be rated X because
they are unhealthy for young children

As a healthy parent I work hard to be certain that
my kids are never exposed to words and pictures
that are unhealthy.

READ MORE ABOUT
Safety

47

My kids don't know what's best. I do.
I know that my kids often want

those things that
are forbidden.

I know that my kids often think that
they can make their own choices.

I know that as a healthy parent I can allow my kids
to make some choices but I am always in charge.

I know that my kids think that violent and
sexual images that bad language and adult
conversations won't bother them.

I know that these things often
give my kids bad dreams
disturb their concentration
cause fears and confusion
and sometimes suggest dangerous actions.
That's why I protect my kids from x-rated media.

READ MORE ABOUT
Zero tolerance · **C**onsistency

48

...or Yummy?

I know that yummy!
is one way that my kids tell me
that something feels good
or looks good
or tastes good.

I know that my job as a healthy parent
is to help my kids discover what is safe
to eat
and touch
and wear
and play with.

I know that my kids like to explore.
I know that my kids want to touch
and eat many things that are not safe.

I know that my job as a healthy parent
is to help my kids learn what really is yummy!

READ MORE ABOUT
Healthy · **If** ... then

49

Yucky!

I know that yucky!
is one way that my kids tell me that
something is new
or ugly
or scary
or doesn't feel right
or doesn't taste right.

I know that my job as a healthy parent is to help my kids
learn to discover what they like and don't like.

I know that my job as a healthy parent is to help my kids
learn how to say what they think and what they feel.

When yucky! means dangerous,
I make certain that my kids are safe.

When yucky! means new I help my kids discover new
things without making it a battle.

READ MORE ABOUT
Battles • **Safety** • **"No!"**

Zero
tolerance

I know that as a healthy parent I try to be patient and understanding and open to new things.

I know as a healthy parent that there are some things that are never okay.

If I have zero tolerance for these things, then my kids may learn zero tolerance for them as well.

I will never allow my child to
disrespect people
harm living creatures
destroy property or
judge others based on skin color, race,
religion, gender or sexual orientation.

I will never allow my home to contain
illegal drugs or alcohol
media that degrades human beings
weapons or illegal activities

Zero tolerance for these things helps to keep my children and my family safe and gives me hope for our future.

 tolerance

 But all the kids do it!

I know that everyone wants to fit in.

I know that peer pressure can make my kids think,
"If I want to fit in then I must do something dangerous."

I know that kids often think that if all the other kids do it then they should, too.

I know as a healthy parent that if I have
zero tolerance
then there is no choice.

We can always talk about it. I can try to understand my child's wishes and choices, but I must stand by my limits firmly and calmly every time.

READ MORE ABOUT
Safety • **"No!"** • **C**onsistency • **A**nchors

PSIA information can be obtained at www.ICGtesting.com
Printed in the USA
/OW06s1457200915

18739BV00006B/35/P

More Great Books from
Unhooked Books

The Complicated Relationships Publisher

Available in paperback and in ebook (digital)
format from booksellers
everywhere

Visit our online bookstore at
www.unhookedbooks.com
Or call 1-888-986-4665